Stitched

ARTISTIC FABRIC PROJECTS FOR YOUR HOME

Christine Morgan

American Quilter's Society
P. O. Box 3290 • Paducah, KY 42002-3290
www.AmericanQuilter.com

Located in Paducah, Kentucky, the American Quilter's Society (AQS) is dedicated to promoting the accomplishments of today's quilters. Through its publications and events, AQS strives to honor today's quiltmakers and their work and to inspire future creativity and innovation in quiltmaking.

EXECUTIVE BOOK EDITOR: ANDI MILAM REYNOLDS
COPY EDITOR: MARILYN KRUSE
GRAPHIC DESIGN: ELAINE WILSON
COVER DESIGN: MICHAEL BUCKINGHAM
PHOTOGRAPHY: CHARLES R. LYNCH
GALLERY PHOTOGRAPHY: CHRISTINE MORGAN

Additional copies of this book may be ordered from the American Quilter's Society, PO Box 3290, Paducah, KY 42002-3290, or online at www.AmericanQuilter.com.

Text © 2012, Author, Christine Morgan
Artwork © 2012, American Quilter's Society

LIBRARY OF CONGRESS CATALOGING-IN-PUBLICATION DATA

Morgan, Christine, 1951 August 26-
   Stacked and stitched : artistic fabric projects for your home / by Christine Morgan.
   80 pages cm
   Summary: "Christine Morgan developed a method that retains the pattern and design of layers rather than obscure them in 'fluffiness' while working with chenille. She calls the layered and slashed fabric 'pelts.' The 'pelts' include bold appliqués and off-center piecing to create pieces of fabric art. Instructions for 4 projects and inspiration gallery included"-- Provided by publisher.
   ISBN 978-1-60460-032-2
   1. Appliqué. 2. Textile crafts. 3. Stitches (Sewing) I. Title.
   TT779.M665 2012
   746--dc23
                              2012029493

OPPOSITE: LEAF table runner, detail. Full table runner on page 39.

LEAF table runner, detail; full table runner
on page 65

Contents

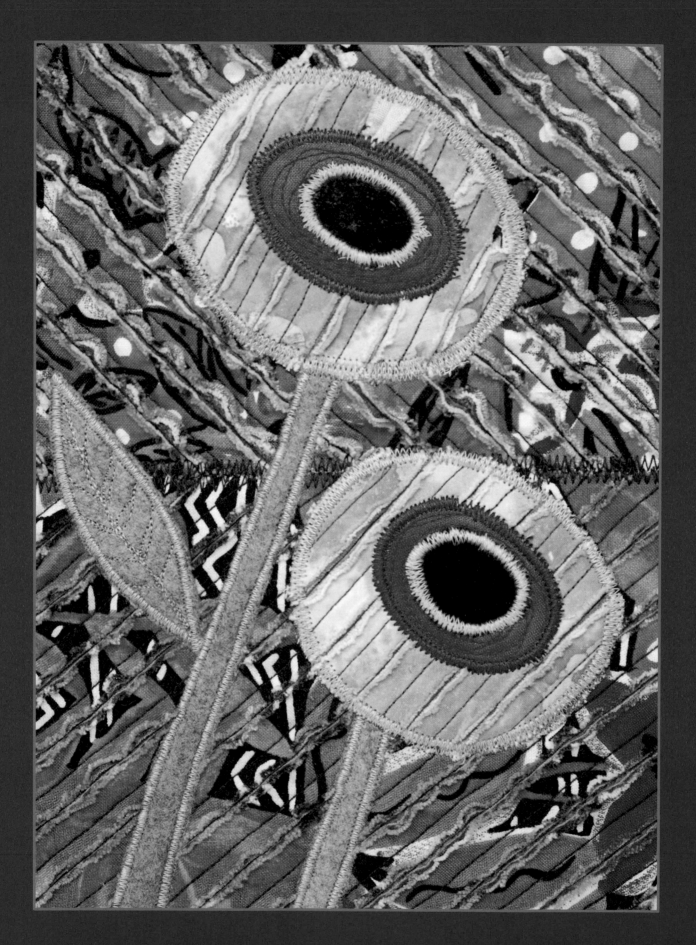

STACKED & Stitched ● *Christine Morgan*

Chapter 1

Introduction to
Stacked and Stitched Pelt Quilts

I have been working with fabric for 30 years, most of that time designing and hand sewing quilts. Eight years ago I was commissioned to create a wallhanging for an office with acoustical issues. I decided on the subject matter—a coral reef—and the sky, water, and fish fabrics I wanted to use.

While I thought about how best to address the acoustical problem, I remembered directions for a vest pattern a friend had shown me a few weeks prior.

I had only glanced at the pattern to be polite—having zero interest in making clothing—but I did get the gist of the technique, which was to layer fabric, sew the layers on the bias, then slash, wash, and dry them to make the fabrics "bloom."

The directions called for a top layer, a layer of white batting, and a bottom layer. I didn't want to use white batting, so I decided to try four layers of regular cotton instead. I worked in 12" squares and sewed them together in a traditional way. I was very pleased with the finished wall hanging.

I had a few 12" squares left over and almost threw them away, but decided to try cutting some shapes out of them. I wasn't sure it would work, but when it did, I started to see the design potential in this technique.

Over the next few months I experimented with everything from raw silk to mosquito netting. The variety of effects, textures, and depth of color achievable was fascinating. I learned which fabrics and fabric combinations worked best for me, and adapted traditional quiltmaking techniques in order to piece and appliqué my designs.

I generally work with ½ yard (approximately 22" x 36") pieces and I call the finished product "fabric pelts" or just "pelts" because of their weight and feel.

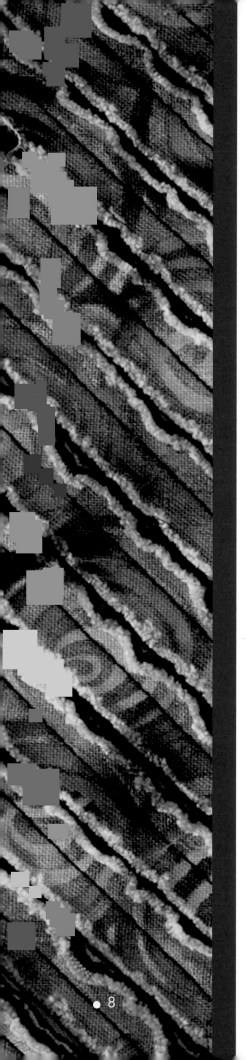

Introduction to Stacked and Stitched Pelt Quilts

Over the years, when people asked me if what I did was faux chenille, I would say 'yes,' but there were those who said it was not faux chenille. I began calling it a "layered and slashed" technique. I recently purchased *Variations in Chenille* by Nanette Holmberg and learned that my process is similar to but definitely not her trademarked "faux chenille." I'm fairly certain that the vest pattern my friend showed me was one of Nanette Holmberg's patterns, and in retrospect, I am glad I wasn't more polite and asked to see what the garment would look like, or I might never have tried creating a similar but different technique.

The main difference between faux chenille and my technique is the look of the finished fabric. I retain the colors and patterns in my top fabrics.

Another difference is that I work with mainly cotton fabrics; faux chenille fabrics are mostly rayons or fabrics that fray so much that the patterns are obscured.

Finally, Ms. Holmberg's focus is wearable art—she creates beautiful fabrics for her clothing. My fabrics not only have a different look, they are also used very differently in creating my designs. I don't have to consider drape or other garment construction limitations, so I can work much more simply with a lot less pinning and sewing in place.

You will not need any special equipment or tools to get started—just a sewing machine that makes straight and zigzag stitches, allows you to drop the feed dogs, and accepts a walking foot to free-motion quilt. I couldn't live without my trusty hatpin and my slash cutting tool, but you can get by with a regular pin and a pair of scissors. A 24" clear acrylic ruler and some masking tape are helpful if you have them.

In a nutshell, this technique involves layering 5 to 7 fabrics (depending on the fiber content; some fabrics count as 2 layers) stacked and sewn on the bias in parallel rows approximately ⅜"–½" apart. You then cut through or slash all but the bottom layer and wash and dry the layers.

Your finished "pelt" is then ready to be cut into whatever size and shape pieces you need.

Trace templates on the wrong side of the pelt, aligning the guidelines with the bias stitching in the direction you want your slashed rows to run. The cut-out pieces are then pinned and zig-zag-stitched to a foundation fabric.

Pelt fabrics lend themselves perfectly to all kinds of home decorating projects. They are durable, functional, easy to care for, and above all, beautiful. Textiles add warmth and personality to any room.

Although the process for making layered and slashed fabrics is labor- and materials-intensive, I think the finished product is well worth the effort because the design possibilities are so rich. I am confident that you will enjoy making and using pelts, too, and will find wonderful and unique ways to work with them.

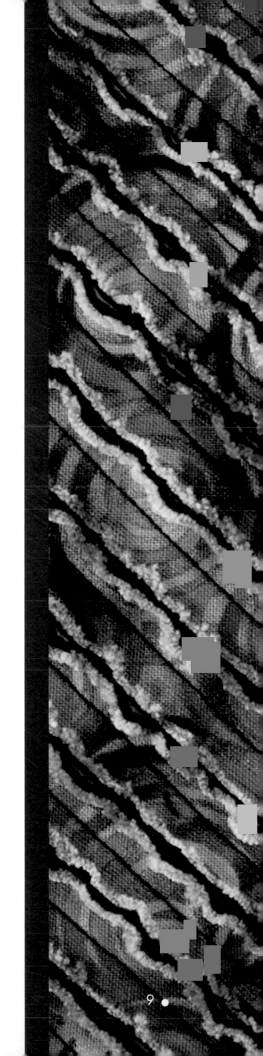

Chapter 2

Choosing
Fabrics for Pelts

What I want to achieve is a balance between preserving the colors and patterns of the top fabric while adding texture and depth by using filler layers to create a nice bloom.

There are some fabrics that work better than others to accomplish this balance in fairly predictable ways, but you won't know for sure until you take the pelt out of the dryer. I think that the element of unpredictability is what keeps me so engaged in this technique.

Even if the result is not what you need for a particular project, I have learned that eventually that pelt will be perfect for something.

There are three types of fabrics you will need: tops, fillers, and bottoms. They each have special requirements.

TOPS

Tops are the stars, the fabrics you love and want to work with. Choose top fabrics for a project exactly like you would for a quilt, according to your own taste and style. There are a few things to keep in mind when shopping for top fabrics:

STACKED & Stitched ◉ *Christine Morgan*

Fiber Content

Medium weight 100 percent cottons are your best choices; they will have a reliable bloom and are available in a glorious array of options.

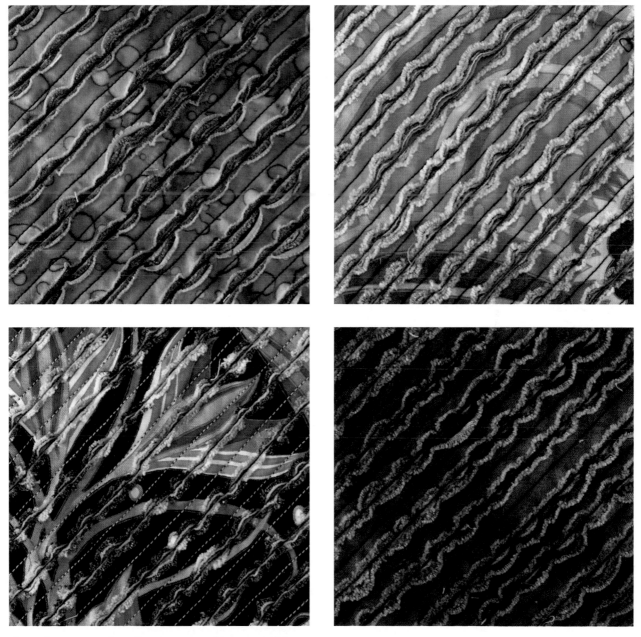

These four examples of cotton tops show good bloom that retains the characteristics of each top fabric.

Choosing Fabrics for Pelts

Lightweight (not sheer) or medium weight 100 percent polyesters are a nice alternative, even though they have almost no bloom; the scale of the prints and vivid colors are sometimes irresistible. These fabrics provide a great punch of color and pattern.

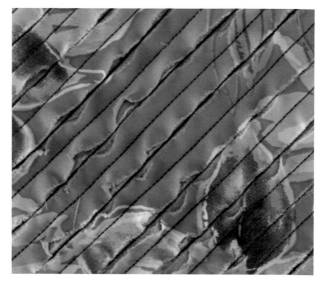

Here are two 100-percent polyester top fabrics. Left is lightweight, right is medium weight.

Medium-weight satins can work well also and have a nice sheen. The bloom will vary, so do a sample block before you make a larger pelt.

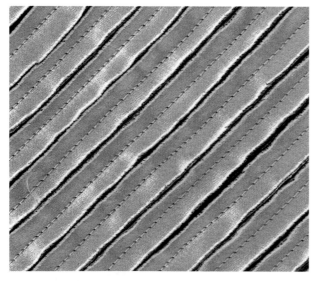
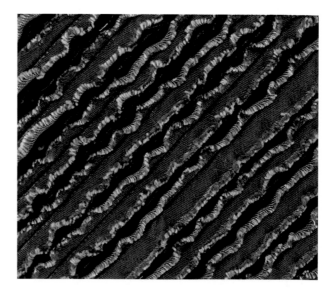

Two examples of satin used as the top fabric

STACKED & Stitched ◉ *Christine Morgan*

Dye Saturation

It's preferable to use fabrics that have dye saturation through to the wrong side for tops; a white back can deaden the colors. I will use fabrics with white backs if I really love them, but I use strong filler fabrics to compensate.

Pattern Scale

Large scale prints work best if your design has large pieces. If you are working with small templates, a large scale pattern can be tricky to use effectively.

Medium scale fabrics work best for me when I want strong patterns visible in my designs.

I use lots of small scale prints. They read as solids from a distance, especially if there isn't much contrast in the print. Small-scale prints with many different colors are very versatile. They allow you to emphasize one of the colors by reinforcing it with your filler fabric choices, and they provide more options when you are piecing them with other fabrics in a design.

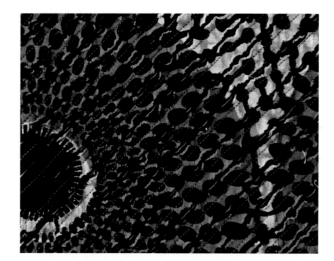

Large scale print

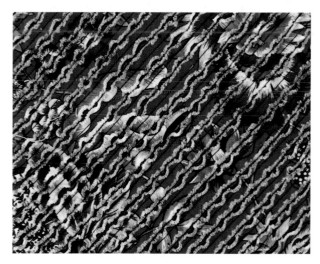

Medium scale print

Small scale print

Fabrics to Avoid for Tops

Rayon and other loose weaves bloom too much and the patterns are lost completely or have a smeary look.

100% Rayon fabric before and after using it as the top fabric in a pelt

Heavy or stiff fabrics are also problematic, but for the opposite reason: They just lie flat and feel stiff after repeated washing and drying.

I very rarely use solid colors as top fabrics, so I guess you could say I avoid them. They just aren't as interesting as something with even a very subtle print. That being said, it is all about fabrics that you are drawn to, so experiment with them regardless of their characteristics. Try some small sample blocks and see what happens.

FILLERS / LAYERS

These fabrics are the supporting cast and are there to enhance the top fabrics, but still have a presence. Good bloom is the key for filler fabrics—that, and good strong color.

Once again, cottons are going to be great choices. Solid color cotton fabrics are affordable, have great dye saturation, and are available in many hues. Stock up on these when you find a deal. Solid color cottons range in weight from thin to thick, which is reflected in the price. They all have their uses in the right combinations. As a rule I count one juicy Kona cotton as two layers because these fabrics have such good bloom they can overwhelm the top fabric if used in more than two layers.

Other single layer choices for great bloom that can count as two layers are dupioni silk, homespun, brushed cotton, cotton gauze, and some flannels.

BOTTOMS

Ideal bottom fabrics are lightweight upholstery/home dec material with strong, bright color on the right side and little or no color saturation through to the wrong side.

These fabrics are not easy to find nor are they always affordable, so I buy them when I find them if the price is right. They are ideal because they are heavy enough to lie flat when you are working with them; this makes them easier to handle when sewing the bias lines. They provide a solid and stable foundation for your pelts if they end up in a rug or table runner, which will be washed and dried repeatedly. The light-colored wrong side allows you to see the sewn bias lines clearly when you are lining up your templates, and also makes it easy to see the traced outlines of your templates so you can cut them out.

Another benefit of a heavier bottom fabric is that it eliminates the "parallelogram effect," which is when your rectangular pelt shrinks during washing and drying and becomes a parallelogram. The pelt can shrink up to 2" out of square on each side. This is not a big issue when you are using small templates, but if your templates are larger, such as the leaf template in Project 3, you will want to compensate for any potential shrinkage by making larger pelts.

When I don't have ideal bottom fabrics—which is most of the time—I opt for inexpensive poly/cotton broadcloth. The best thing about these fabrics is the intense colors available; what they lack in interesting patterns is made up for in glow.

Ideal bottom fabric is a lightweight upholstery fabric with strong color on the right side and almost white on the wrong side.

Rectangular or square pelts can shrink up to 2" out of square on each side after washing and drying, resulting in a parallelogram.

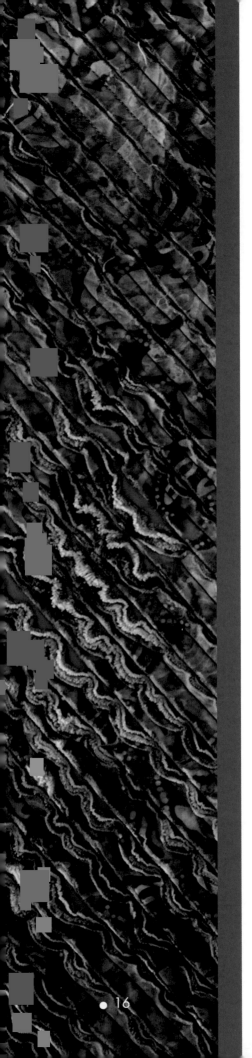

Choosing Fabrics for Pelts

I became obsessed with glow after attending a Renoir exhibit and experiencing the light radiating from his paintings. I don't know how Renoir achieved his glow, but I try to get a glow by using a brightly colored bottom fabric when it's appropriate.

If you have a good candidate for bottom fabric but it has a very dark or patterned wrong side (which will make seeing markings difficult), add a layer of muslin or any lightweight, light-colored fabric behind it.

Just remember that although bloom isn't a concern for the bottom fabric, this layer may be visible to some degree and needs to harmonize with the other fabrics.

SUGGESTIONS FOR COMBINING FABRICS FOR PELTS

There are different strategies for selecting and using prints and solids (which include small-scale prints or batiks that will read as solids). In both cases I choose my top and bottom fabrics first and then audition filler fabrics that harmonize with both the top and bottom fabrics.

Prints

When working with a print, my main objective is to maintain the integrity of the print while adding some pizzazz. I pull colors right out of the top fabric for the filler layers, and I like to add some sparkle by placing a very bright color in the layer directly under the top fabric.

The slashing process breaks up the print and mutes it a bit, so I like to pump the volume back up with a strong color just behind it. If I have chosen a dark bottom layer, I want to put a lighter layer on top of it for some contrast.

LEFT: Sample showing dark/light fabric use.

STACKED & Stitched ⊡ *Christine Morgan*

To help keep my print design crisp and well delineated, I want to make sure that there is at least one lighter layer under dark areas and one darker layer under the light areas of the print. This also makes your slash lines more visible.

Solids

When I work with a top fabric that reads "solid," I just want to intensify the colors that are already in the fabric, or intensify one or more of them to shift the color in that direction.

For example, if I am using a batik as my top fabric and it is predominantly yellow with hints of orange and ocher, I might use orange in two of my filler layers to shift the overall color to a yellow-orange.

Avoid mixing too many contrasting colors into your pelts or your colors will become muddy and dull. Avoid mixing too many bold prints, also. Although you can get some interesting effects, mostly you just get an unattractive mishmash.

Examples

When I first got involved with this technique I did a lot of experimentation and documented the results. What I discovered was that each fabric would react in a unique way with the other fabrics. There were just too many variables to make it 100 percent predictable, and that's just fine with me. It keeps the process fresh and exciting. On pages 18–19 are some examples of combinations that work for me in achieving the looks that I want; they will serve as a guide in helping you get the looks that appeal to you.

RIGHT: Sample showing solid-type yellow top fabric

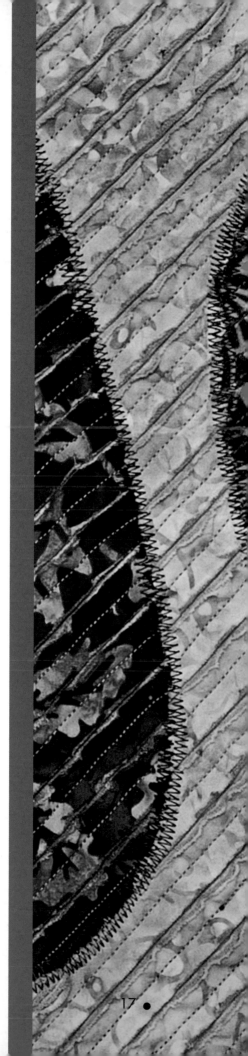

Choosing Fabrics for Pelts

I have used the same top fabric, a green-and-gold cotton batik, in each of the first six examples that follow to illustrate how different fabrics bloom and how color and pattern choices affect the look of the finished pelt. The variation in number of fabrics per example is due to different fabric weights; aim for 5 to 7 fabrics per pelt as you experiment. In the layers listed on the following pages, a (2) beside a layer indicates it counts as two fabrics.

RIGHT: Six pelts with the same top fabric

STACKED & Stitched ◉ *Christine Morgan*

Example 1

Objective: *Illustrate how a bold, high contrast print in layer 2 can affect the top fabric.*

TOP – green gold cotton batik
Large scale heavy cotton green gold print (2)
Light green Kona cotton (2)
Green cotton
BOTTOM – yellow poly/cotton broadcloth

RIGHT: The bold, high contrast print in layer 2 adds an additional pattern of light and dark areas.

This area has been brushed to bloom.

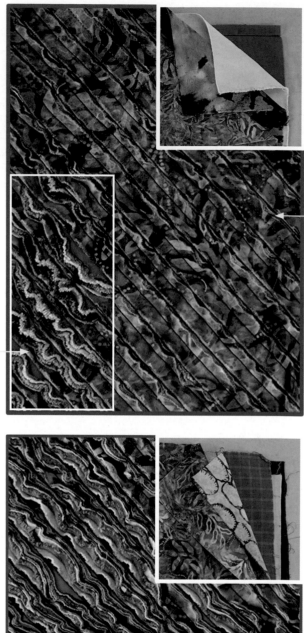

Unbrushed area

Example 2

Objective: *Illustrate the bloom of brushed cotton and overall color shift to gold.*

Top – green gold cotton batik
Yellow green cotton batik
Gold brushed cotton plaid (2)
Yellow cotton
Dark olive green cotton
BOTTOM – yellow poly/cotton broadcloth

RIGHT: The bloom almost overwhelms the pattern on the top fabric, but it makes the pelt very soft and is perfect for pillow tops.

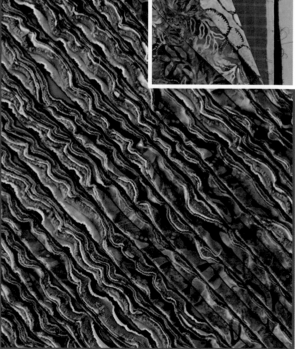

STACKED & Stitched ● *Christine Morgan*

Example 3

Objective: Illustrate the look and bloom of dupioni silk in layer 2.

TOP – green gold cotton batik
Green dupioni silk (2)
Yellow cotton
Gold cotton
Dark green dragonfly cotton print
BOTTOM – yellow poly/cotton broadcloth

RIGHT: The silk just shimmers and adds richness to the look of the pelt. Real dupioni silk has a rough texture and a papery feel that adds to the whole pelt experience. I used it a lot more when it was $15 per yard but I use it less often now that it is $28 or more per yard.

Example 4

Objective: Illustrate the bloom of flannel and color shift to green.

TOP – green gold cotton batik
Yellow cotton
Green flannel (2)
Dark green dragonfly printed cotton
Green cotton
BOTTOM – yellow poly/cotton broadcloth

RIGHT: The bloom of the flannel does overwhelm the top fabric, but it makes the pelt very soft.

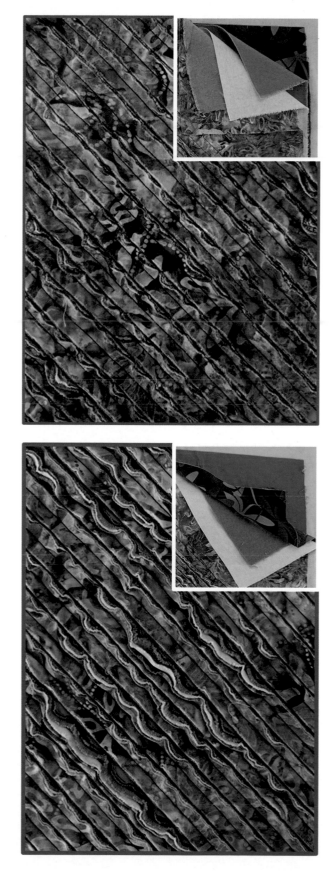

Example 5

Objective: Show the color shift to orange.

TOP – green gold cotton batik
Orange cotton
Yellow Kona cotton (2)
Burnt orange cotton
Brown and orange cotton batik
BOTTOM – yellow poly/cotton broadcloth

RIGHT: Note how the overall color shifts to orange.

Example 6

Objective: Show the color shift to violet.

TOP – green gold cotton batik
Violet/yellow/green geometric cotton print
Light violet Kona cotton (2)
Dark violet cotton
Green cotton
BOTTOM – violet poly/cotton broadcloth

RIGHT AND BELOW: Note how the use of a three-color print changes the look altogether and shifts the color to violet.

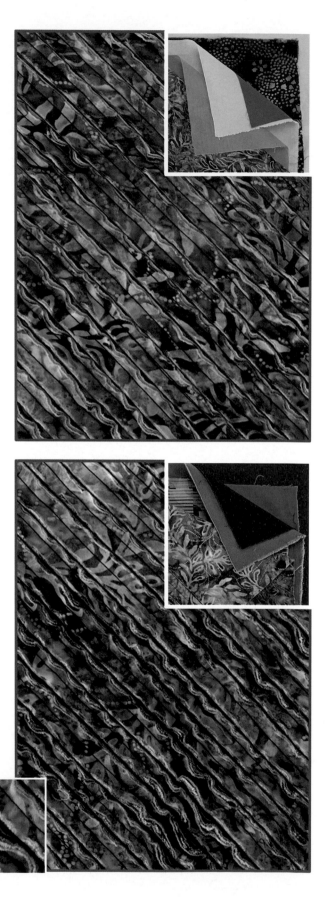

STACKED & Stitched ◙ *Christine Morgan*

Examples 7 and 8 have the same top fabric—a dark violet and red floral cotton print.

Example 7

Objective: *Shift the color to red violet.*

TOP – dark violet and red floral cotton print
Red cotton
Red violet cotton batik
Dark red cotton
Red Kona cotton (2)
BOTTOM – violet poly/cotton broadcloth

RIGHT: All these red layers push the contrast with the violet top fabric.

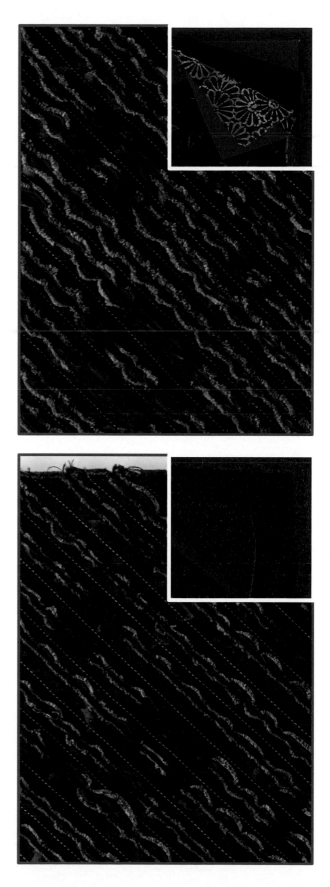

Example 8

Objective: *Lighten and brighten the top fabric but still keep the overall tone dark.*

TOP – dark violet and red floral cotton print
Bright red and black cotton print
Dark violet Kona cotton (2)
Dark red cotton
Dark red cotton
BOTTOM – violet poly/cotton broadcloth

RIGHT: The white selvage border can be cut off, or, as I did here, placed at the top of the pelt where it will be cut off eventually. It provides a straight line to use when marking the 45-degree angle for the bias lines.

Example 9

Objective: *This top fabric has very dark and very light areas. I wanted to lighten the dark areas and darken the light areas by using a mix of light and dark fabrics as filler fabrics.*

TOP – green, red violet, and blue green
cotton batik
Yellow cotton
Orange Kona cotton (2)
Yellow cotton
Yellow orange Kona cotton
BOTTOM – green poly/cotton broadcloth

RIGHT: See the importance of the bottom layer color.

Example 10

Objective: *Preserve the top fabric pattern while adding filler fabrics with just enough bloom to make the slash line visible.*

TOP – medium scale floral cotton print
Yellow cotton
Red orange Kona cotton (2)
Yellow ocher Kona cotton (2)
BOTTOM – violet poly/cotton broadcloth

RIGHT: Select closely matching fabrics to the top fabric to preserve its pattern.

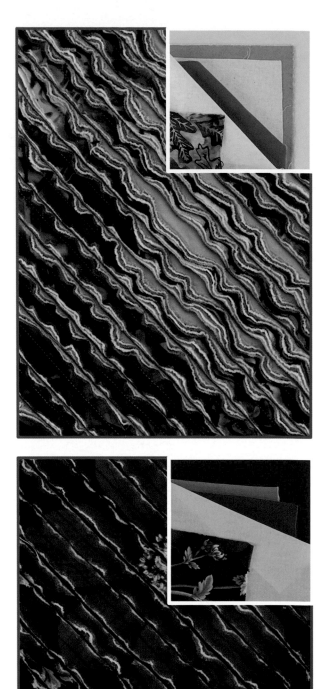

STACKED & Stitched ⊡ *Christine Morgan*

Example 11

Objective: Get as much bloom as possible without adding too much bulk.

TOP – 100% polyester floral print
Yellow cotton
Green and black heavy cotton print
Orange heavy cotton print (wrong side up)
Green and black heavy cotton print
BOTTOM – "ideal" medium weight
    upholstery fabric

RIGHT: Use high blooming filler fabrics under polyester, which has little or no bloom.

Example 12

Objective: I only want to enhance this beautiful fabric by adding a little texture.

TOP – African print cotton
Black Kona cotton (2)
Red cotton
Black Kona cotton (2)
Dark red cotton print

RIGHT: I would probably use this fabric by itself as a pillow top or in something with large pattern pieces.

Chapter 3

Making Pelts

WHAT IS A PELT?

Pelts consist of a bottom fabric, 3 to 5 filler layers, and a top fabric. These fabrics are sewn together with parallel rows of stitching on the bias. The stitching creates channels that are slashed through except for the bottom fabric, which holds the pelt together. The pelt is then washed and dried, causing the fabrics to bloom.

The finished look of the pelt will be determined by the fiber content, color, pattern, position in the layers, and weave of the fabrics you have chosen. Therein lies the art and excitement of this technique.

Front detail of a pelt

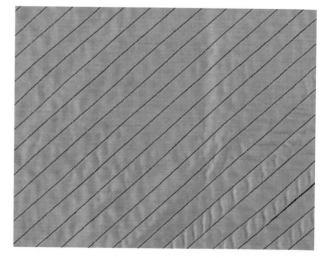

Back detail of a pelt

STACKED & Stitched ◙ *Christine Morgan*

WHAT SIZE SHOULD PELTS BE?

For the first piece I made using this technique, I worked with 12" x 12" squares that I then joined together. I realized later that I could make larger pelts and cut out the shapes I needed.

I usually work with ½ yard of fabric, or pieces approximately 22" x 36". The largest pelt I have attempted was 36" x 36". It was doable but unwieldy. I suggest that you experiment with a couple of 12" x 12" pieces and then work with ¼ yard or approximately 18" x 22" pelts.

There are many things you can make with extra pelts. I save all my scraps and make coasters or table toppers, or combine them in larger projects that call for small pieces.

I have specified the minimum sizes of all pelts you will need for the projects in this book if you choose to make only the pelts you need. Working in ½ or ¼ yard pieces is efficient, makes it easy to figure out how much yardage you need, and saves you from amassing heaps of odds and ends.

HOW FAR APART SHOULD THE ROWS BE?

I make my rows ⅜" to ½" apart, but you can go as wide or as narrow as you want, as long as you can fit a scissors or a slash cutter in the channel to cut them. Slight variations in the width won't be noticeable, but big variations will be, so try and keep your rows as consistent as you can.

WHAT KIND OF THREAD SHOULD BE USED?

I use whatever I can find, as long as it is good quality. I never know whether the pelt I am making is going to end up as a rug and get washed repeatedly, so I make them all as durable as possible. The most important consideration in choosing your top

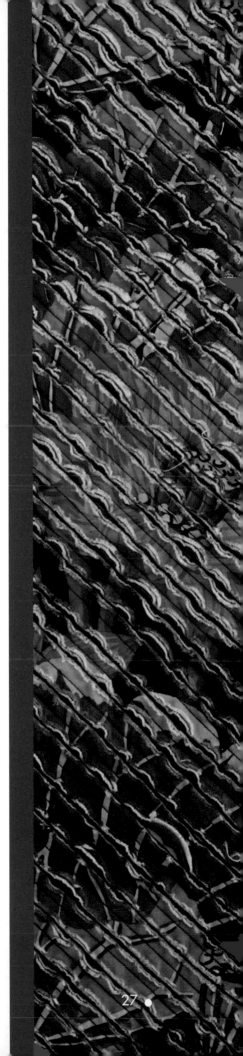

thread color is that you can see it easily against your top fabric. When you are sewing the parallel rows, these stitches will be your guide from one row to the next and you will need to see them clearly. The bobbin thread should be easily seen against the wrong side of your bottom fabric. You will be using these stitches to line up your templates.

STEP-BY-STEP DIRECTIONS FOR MAKING AN 18" X 21" PELT

You will need:

> 21" x 24" bottom fabric
>
> 3 to 5 pieces 18" x 21" of filler/layer fabrics (I used 2 Kona cottons that I counted as a total of 3 layers)
>
> 18" x 21" top fabric
>
> 3" x 24" or 6" x 24" clear acrylic ruler with 45-degree angle marking
>
> iron
>
> masking tape
>
> scissors and/or slash cutter tool

Step 1. Assemble your fabrics right sides up (cut to correct sizes) and determine their order from bottom fabric to top fabric. Iron each fabric as you go; get out any big creases that could cause gapping in the finished pelt.

Lay out your bottom fabric and then place your first layer in the center. You want at least a 1" border on all sides of the first layer. This border is important; it allows you to oversew the

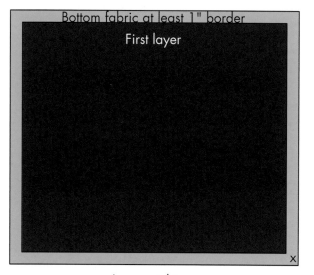

Bottom fabric at least 1" border

First layer

x

x = Lower right corner

Fig. 3–1. Place the first layer fabric in the center of the bottom layer.

parallel rows, which is faster than trying to stop at the edges. This border gives you something to adhere the masking tape to, and it provides a platform for your scissors to bite into when you are cutting the channels. (Fig. 3–1).

Step 2. Offset the second layer. You want to see just a peek, ⅛"–¼", of the first layer showing at the bottom and right side. This will ensure that you get the scissors under that first layer (Fig. 3–2).

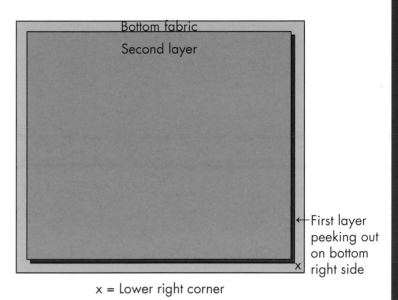

x = Lower right corner

Fig. 3–2. Offset the second layer on the first layer.

Step 3. Add the remaining layers and top fabric directly on top of the second layer. Place the ruler on top of the stack and line up the 45-degree angle marking with the selvage edge (Fig. 3–3).

Step 4. Run masking tape along the edge of the ruler, extending onto the border at the top and bottom. Remove the ruler and pin along the edge of the tape; 5 or 6 pins is plenty (Fig. 3–3).

Put a pin in the lower left corner and the upper right corner. These pins will keep the layers in place while you sew the parallel rows; they may need to be readjusted as you sew. Remove them when you get close to the corners.

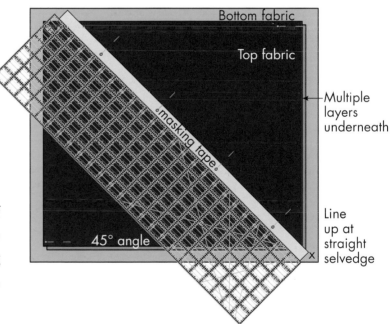

Fig. 3–3. Use the 45-degree angle on the ruler to establish the bias line for stitching.

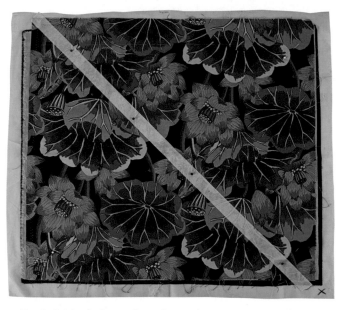

Fig. 3–4. Mark the pelt with masking tape to indicate the bias line, pin the pelt, and mark the lower right corner.

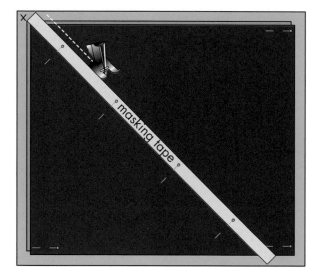

Fig. 3–5. Establish the first row of stitches along the masking tape edge opposite the pins.

Mark an X in the lower right corner so you can position the pelt when you are ready to slash (Fig. 3–4).

Step 5. The pelt is now ready to sew. Use a straight stitch with a length of 2.0. Line up the presser foot with the edge of the masking tape opposite the pins and sew the first row (Fig. 3–5).

Step 6. With the needle down, raise the presser foot and rotate the pelt counterclockwise 180 degrees. Raise the needle and reposition the pelt ⅜"–½" to the left; you will alternate moving to left and right with each row of stitching (Fig. 3–6).

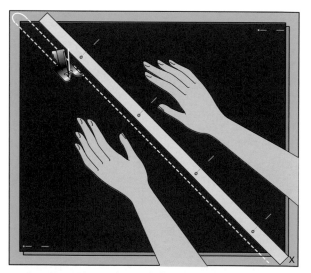

Fig. 3–6. Reposition the pelt for the next row of stitches. Smooth the fabric with your palms as you sew. Remove the pins.

NOTE: The knee control for raising and lowering the presser foot is very helpful. It allows you to keep both hands free to move the pelt around and keep it smooth as you sew. You can remove the pins along the masking tape now that your bias line is sewn.

Fig. 3 7. Remove the masking tape after you have sewn to the corner.

Step 7. Continue sewing in parallel rows until you reach the corner. Remove the masking tape (Fig. 3–7)

Step 8. Continue sewing parallel rows to the opposite corner rotating the pelt as in Step 6. When all your rows are completed, trim away the border to the edge of the top fabric on the left side and the top of the pelt (Fig. 3–8). This would eventually be cut anyway, but doing it now removes all the thread loops created by repositioning the needle. These loops can snag your slash cutter.

Fig. 3–8. All the rows are sewn, and the top and left edges have been trimmed.

Step 9. Using scissors, start cutting each row. Just a few snips or approximately 2" to 3" will do. You can use the slash cutter to start the rows (although scissors are easier) but once they are started, it works well. Do not cut the bottom layer.

When you have cut all your rows, you can start slashing. If your blade is sharp, this should

Fig. 3–9. All rows have been cut. Some of the channels are slashed. Note how the hand keeps tension on the pelt to help keep the slash in the center of the row.

be almost effortless. Keep the cut in the center of the channel. Keep tension on the pelt as you slash by pressing down with your hand and following the slash cutter; this will help keep the cut in the center of the channel (Fig. 3–9).

Step 10. When all rows are slashed, trim the bottom and right edges (Figs. 3–10 and 3–11).

Step 11. With the wrong side facing up, stitch around the perimeter of the pelt, ⅛" – ¼" from the edge. This will secure the rows of stitching as you wash and dry the pelt (Fig. 3–12.

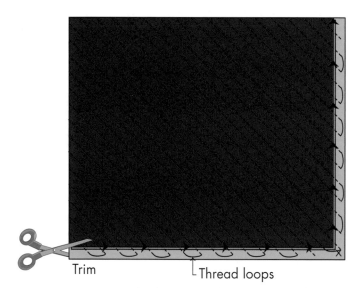

Trim   └Thread loops

Fig. 3–10. Trim the bottom and right edges after all of the rows are slashed.

Fig. 3–11. This pelt is complete and trimmed.

Step 12. Wash and dry the pelt. Wash it in cold water, use a normal setting, and add a splash of detergent. Don't overload the washer. Dry on normal temperature. Check and clean the lint filter frequently, as lots of lint is created. Don't over dry; it can cause the fabrics to bloom too much.

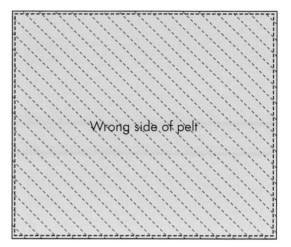

Fig. 3–12. Stitch around the pelt's perimeter so it can be safely washed, dried, and allowed to bloom.

Aside: I recently purchased a low water, energy efficient, top-loading washer. It doesn't have an agitator and the lid locks. I find that very suspicious; I can't watch what it does to move the wash around. Anyway, I hate this washer. It over-agitates some areas on the pelt and under-agitates other areas. Very annoying. I live in hope that one day it will spin with enough velocity to break free of Earth's gravitational pull and fulfill its destiny as space junk.

Finish the pelt correctly by washing it in cold water and drying it just enough, but not too much.

Chapter 4

Tips

The techniques I developed for working with these layered and slashed fabrics grew directly from the traditional quilt making techniques I had been working with for many years. I just made it up as I went along, but I am hoping the adaptations I have come up with will make sense to you and be easy for you to master.

PIECING WITH PELTS

After your pieces have been cut out and pinned to the foundation fabric, join them and secure them to the foundation fabric by basting with a zigzag stitch (W 5.0, L 2.0). I use a hatpin to hold the layers down so the presser foot doesn't fold them open. Stay just a little ahead of the presser foot. The hatpin or a similar tool is also great for poking and prodding things into alignment as you sew. Remove pins as you go; because of the bulkiness of the pelts, the pins can cause a little distortion and you want to keep everything flat.

When all of your seams are basted, zigzag stitch (W 4.2, L 1.2) on both sides of the seam to ensure that everything is secured. I prefer the look of dark thread for both basting and sewing; it helps to delineate each shape and tighten the design.

APPLIQUÉ

Some of the elements I appliqué, such as flower petals or ginkgo leaves, are free-motion quilted before I cut out the shapes. I use a felt similar in color to the top fabric instead of batting to back the fabric and make a whole sheet of petals or leaves. Other elements, such as flower centers, I iron onto fusible interfacing to make them sturdier and easier to work with.

To appliqué the shapes, I zigzag stitch around the perimeter, focusing on attaching the shapes to the background, and then zigzag stitch around again, focusing on covering the raw edge. **It was a big day when I realized I could appliqué one pelt on top of another.** Prior to that I had been inlaying everything because I thought it would be too bulky and hadn't even tried to do it. My mom was right: "You don't know until you try."

FOUNDATION FABRIC

The ideal foundation fabric is a light-colored (at least on one side), lightweight upholstery or home decorating fabric. Avoid anything too flimsy or anything with stretch. You will be attaching all of the pelt pieces to this fabric, so it needs to be fairly sturdy without adding a lot of bulk. I keep an eye out for very inexpensive, misprinted, or just very ugly fabrics to use for foundation fabrics, and I always pre-wash them in case I use them in something I want to be washable.

The light color is preferable because you will be drawing your design on the foundation fabric. The drawing is just a guide; don't try to mash your pieces into the pre-drawn spaces. The layered and slashed pieces will grow a little no matter how carefully you have cut them out. The growth is negligible and becomes an issue only if you are mounting the piece on stretcher strips. In that case, I square up and trim the piece to the correct size before sewing on the border strips.

I am a stickler about trimming threads, locking in stitches, and keeping my sewing machine lint free, but otherwise, I relax and enjoy.

One of the things I really like about my designs is that they often combine different elements, so I have a lot of options when I have a day to do whatever I feel like doing. I have a stack of top fabrics ready to be made into pelts, and a stack of pelts ready to have the bias rows stitched. I can put on some music and free-motion a sheet of flower petals or ginkgo leaves. There is a lot of variety, so if I'm not feeling creative, there are plenty of things I can do to keep busy.

Chapter 5

Templates

I make my templates out of poster board or, if it is something I'm going to use repeatedly, out of mat board or cardboard. See-through template plastic works, too. No matter the material you use, it's important that your templates are accurately drawn and carefully cut out and traced.

I add directional guidelines to all my opaque templates. I consider the direction the bias rows will run in my designs, and I like to change the direction whenever possible. The guidelines on the templates are aligned with the bias stitching on the wrong side of the pelts.

The guidelines represent the direction you want the slashed bias lines to run and are drawn at a 45- or 90-degree angle to the straight edge of the template or any other direction you want.

I also add some lines parallel to the angle markings closer to the corners or edges of the templates to make it easier to check that I am on the same line. These guidelines do not have to fall on the stitching line; they just must be parallel with it. NOTE: These shorter parallel lines are just randomly placed (Fig. 5–1, page 37).

Since you will be tracing the templates on the wrong side of the pelts, you have to remember the slash running down the center of each row of bias stitching on the right side.

When you align templates, try not to allow the edges of the templates to extend past the middle of the row or you will lose all of the filler layers on the other side of the slash. You will lose bits and pieces here and there, but the bottom layer will still be intact, and you will be sewing over these areas, so they won't be very noticeable.

The other thing to keep in mind is to position the templates in a way that will maximize the pelt surface. Share cutting lines when possible, but be careful not to accidentally overlap (Fig. 5–2).

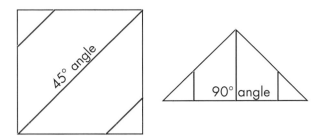

Fig. 5–1. To make and use guidelines, give square templates a 45-degree guideline and triangular templates a 90-degree guideline. Shorter lines, closer to corners, help ensure that you are in correct alignment, i.e., running parallel to the bias stitching lines when tracing templates on the wrong side of the pelt.

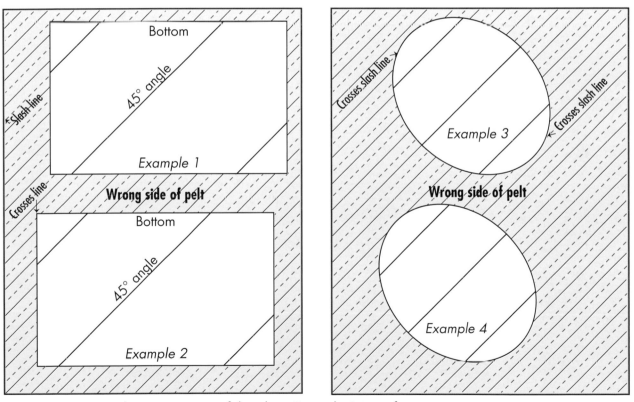

Fig. 5–2. Position templates to minimize fabric loss. Example 1 is preferable; the corners fall right at the slash line. In example 2, the top left corner extends beyond the slash line. Of examples 3 and 4, example 4 is the better choice; the curves do not extend beyond the slash lines like they do in Example 3.

Templates

Templates which have a curve—such as the leaf template in Project 3—should be placed by first positioning the curve as close to the center slash line as possible without extending past it, and then lining up the template accordingly (Fig. 5–3).

In Projects 2 and 3 there are identical templates positioned at right angles to each other so that the bias stitching lines run in opposite directions. When placed side by side, they create a 90-dgree chevron (Figs. 5–4a, b, and c).

Tip: It is important to label your templates in a way that makes sense to you. Because you are tracing the templates on the wrong side of the pelts, when you turn them to the right side, the bias lines will run in the opposite direction and it's easy to be confused.

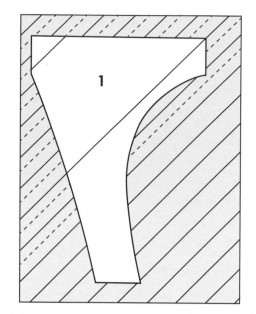

Fig. 5–3. To use curved templates, place templates such as this leaf with the curve positioned first.

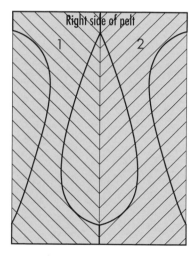

Fig. 5–4b

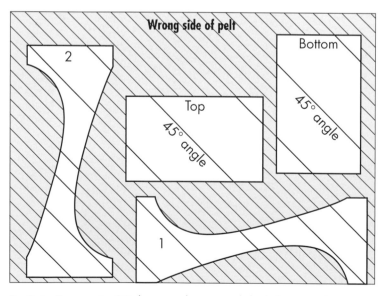

Fig. 5–4a. To create 90-degree chevrons, label the templates so they will be positioned at right angles to each other. Turn them to the right side and place them together.

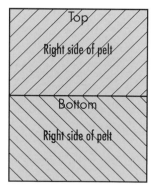

Fig. 5–4c

STACKED & Stitched ⊙ *Christine Morgan*

Chapter 6 **Gallery**

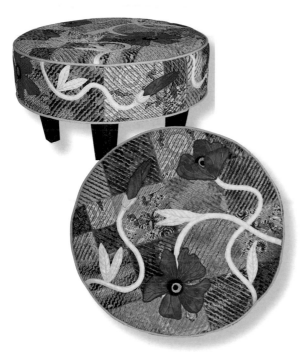

24" Round Poppy ottoman, top and side view

Handbag

24" Round Forest ottoman, side view

Leaf table runner, 48½" x 13½"

Gallery

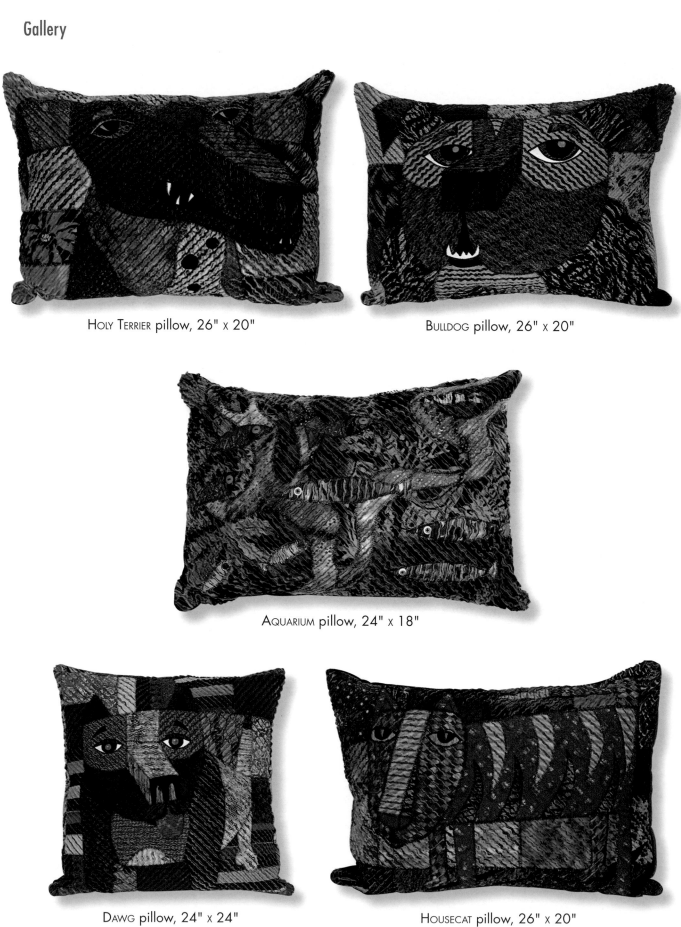

Holy Terrier pillow, 26" x 20"

Bulldog pillow, 26" x 20"

Aquarium pillow, 24" x 18"

Dawg pillow, 24" x 24"

Housecat pillow, 26" x 20"

STACKED & Stitched ◙ Christine Morgan

ORANGE POPPY pillow, 24" x 24"

Pillow, 24" x 12"

SQUARE DANCE pillow, 26" x 20"

Pillow, 24" x 12"

CROCUS pillow, 18" x 18"

Gallery

Sea of Cortez wall quilt, 50" x 50"

Not So Still Life wall quilt, 28" x 46"

Still Life wall quilt, 24" x 24"

Ginkgo pillow, 16" x 16"

STACKED & Stitched ◙ Christine Morgan

Wild Flowers pillow, 24" x 12"

Pansy pillow, 24" x 24"

Ginkgo pillow, 24" x 12"

Sunflowers pillow, 24" x 24"

Pansy pillow top, 24" x 12"

Christine Morgan ● STACKED & Stitched

Chapter 7   Projects

Project 1: **POLLINATION,** 12" x 12" pillow

This project uses only 2 pelts, so choose good, strong top fabrics for both.

STACKED & Stitched ◉ Christine Morgan

Project 1: **POLLINATION PILLOW**

12" x 12" pillow

You will need:

- 2 finished, squared pelts at least 12" x 12" each
- 15" x 15" foundation fabric
- 14" x 27" fabric for pillow case
- 14" x 19" fabric for pillow case lining (optional)
- Thread (black)
- 2 templates (page 50)
- 12" x 12" pillow form

> **Tip:** If you want to make your pillow-case washable, prewash all the fabrics before you cut them.

Step 1. Draw the design on foundation fabric with a 1½" border around it (Fig. 7–1).

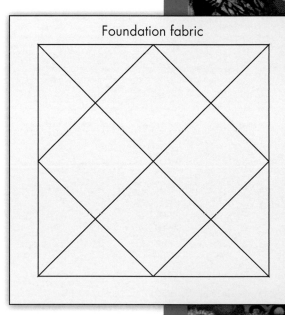

Foundation fabric

Fig. 7–1

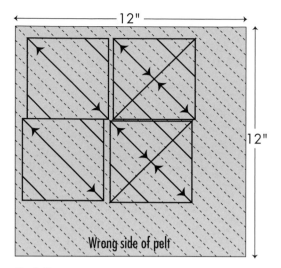

Fig. 7–2

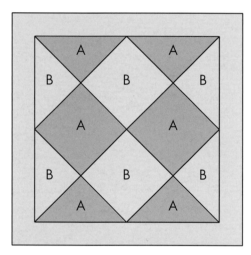

Fig. 7–3

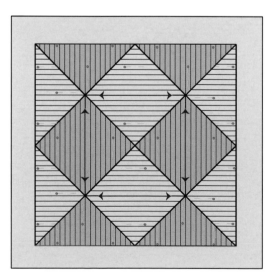

Fig. 7–4

Step 2. Trace templates on the wrong side of each of the two pelts. Make 2 squares and 4 triangles per pelt for a total of 12 shapes. Line up the guidelines on the templates with the bias stitching lines on the pelt back (Fig. 7–2).

Step 3. Cut out all 12 shapes.

Step 4. Arrange pieces until you are happy with the look. I find a design wall invaluable for this stage. I can just pin things up, stand back to look at them, and rearrange pieces easily. Calling one pelt A and the other B, the configuration is as shown in figure 7–3.

Step 5. When you are happy with the arrangement of all of the pieces, pin them to the foundation fabric. Check to make sure the slash lines of the center squares are turned at right angles to one another (Fig. 7–4).

Step 6. Baste all seams with a zigzag stitch (W 5.0, L 2.0), starting in the center and working toward the corners for diagonals, and then baste the interior square. The basting stitch should straddle the seam and hold both pieces in place. Keep your pieces lined up and remove pins as you go to prevent distortion (Figs. 7–5a and b, page 47).

STACKED & Stitched ● *Christine Morgan*

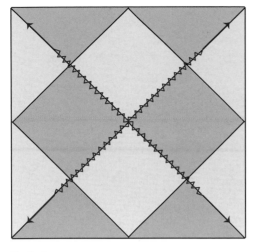

Fig. 7–5a

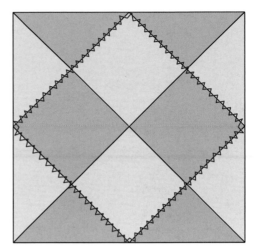

Fig. 7–5b

Step 7. Sew on both sides of all basted seams with a zigzag stitch (W 4.2, L 1.2) (Fig. 7–6).

Step 8. Remove any remaining pins and iron on the wrong side to ease any slight puckering.

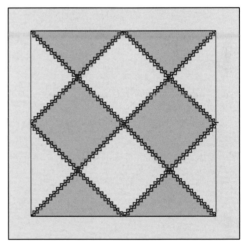

Fig. 7–6

Step 9. Baste around the perimeter with a zigzag stitch (W 5.0, L 2.0) (Fig. 7–7).

Step 10. Make a pillowcase using the pieced pelt:

- Cut 1 piece of lining (optional) 12" x 14" and 1 piece 7" x 14"
- Cut 2 pieces for the pillow back: 1 piece 14" x 16" and 1 piece 14" x 11"
- Mark the fold lines on the wrong side of the pillow back pieces as shown in figures 7–8a–d, page 48.

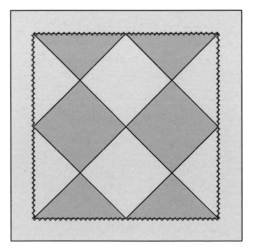

Fig. 7–7

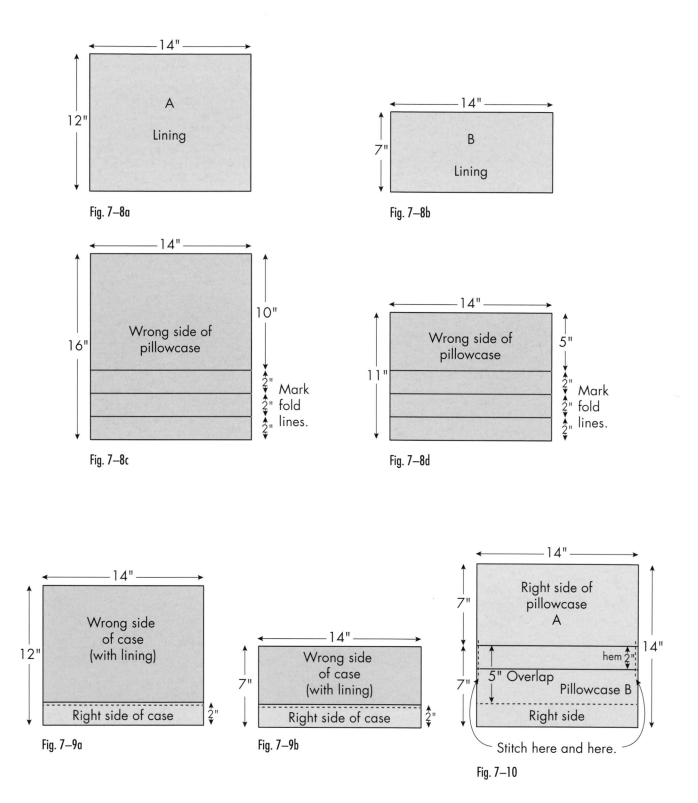

14"

A
Lining

12"

Fig. 7–8a

14"

B
Lining

7"

Fig. 7–8b

14"

Wrong side of pillowcase

16"

10"

2" Mark
2" fold
2" lines.

Fig. 7–8c

14"

Wrong side of pillowcase

11"

5"

2" Mark
2" fold
2" lines.

Fig. 7–8d

14"

Wrong side
of case
(with lining)

12"

Right side of case

2"

Fig. 7–9a

14"

Wrong side
of case
(with lining)

7"

Right side of case

2"

Fig. 7–9b

14"

Right side of
pillowcase
A

7"

14"

hem 2"

5" Overlap

Pillowcase B

7"

Right side

Stitch here and here.

Fig. 7–10

Position the lining in place and iron in the folds. Then straight stitch the back and the lining together (Figs. 7–9a–b, page 48).

With the right sides facing up, place piece B (finished size 14" x 7") on top of piece A (finished size 14" x 12") forming a 14" x 14" square; there will be a 5" overlap of B over A. Straight stitch to hold the pieces in place as shown in figure 7– 10, page 48.

Step 11. Pin the pillowcase and pillow top right sides together. Use the zigzag perimeter stitching on the pillow top back as your guide when pinning. Straight stitch all around (Fig. 7–11).

Step 12. Serge or stabilize the edges and trim excess fabric (Fig. 7–12).

Step 13. Turn the pillowcase right-side out, poking out the corners (I use the rounded end of an old artist's brush) and insert the pillow form (Fig. 7–13).

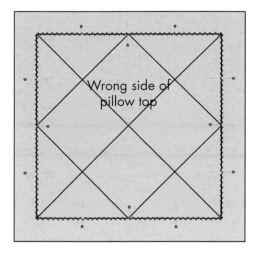

Fig. 7–11

Fig. 7–12

Fig. 7–13

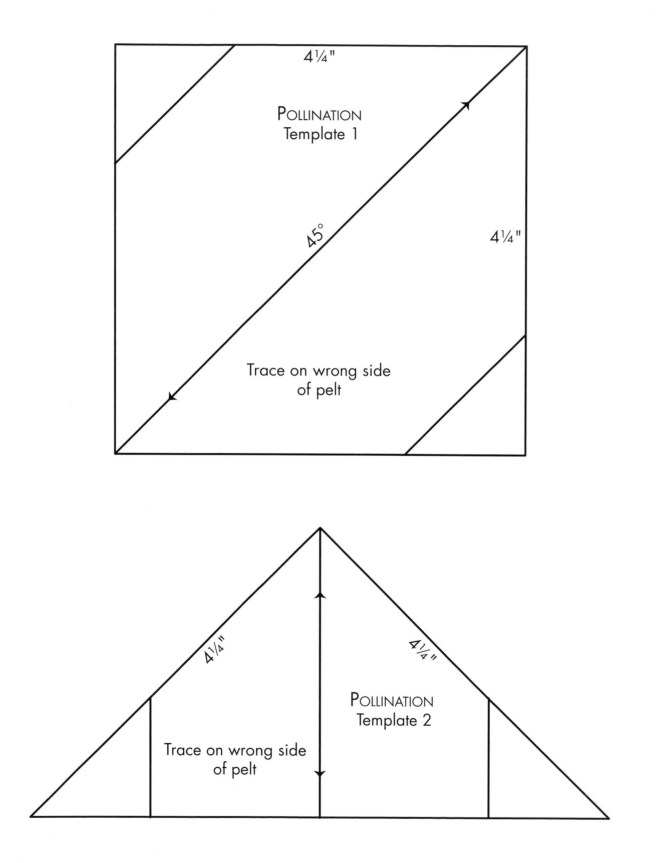

Project 2: FLOWER, 8" x 10" Mini Wallhanging

I like to use bright cheerful colors in these little wallhangings.
They make great gifts, so consider making more than one.

Christine Morgan ⬛ STACKED & Stitched

51 ●

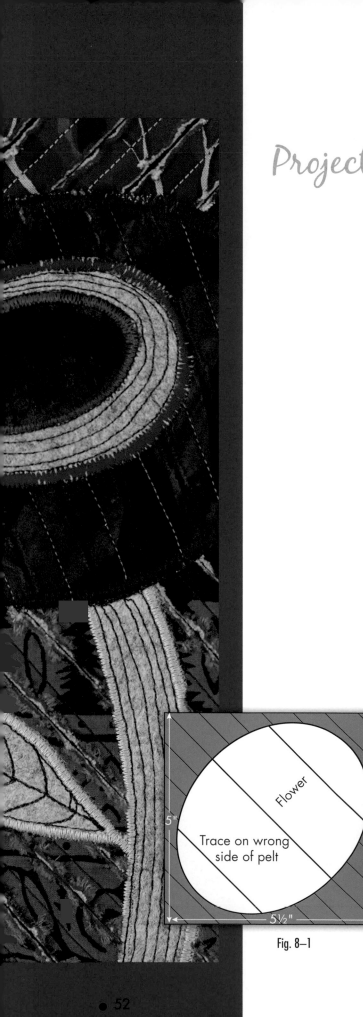

Project 2: FLOWER Mini Wallhanging

8" x 10" Mini Wallhanging

I have organized the construction into 4 parts:
1. **Flower**
2. **Background**
3. **Frame**
4. **Construction**

1. FLOWER

You will need:

- 6 templates (pages 58–59)
- 1 finished, squared pelt at least 5½" x 5½" for a flower
- 4" x 11" fabric for stem, leaves, and flower center (I used a lightly bleached moss green WoolFelt™)
- 2" x 2½" fabric for flower center middle (I used a silk velvet)
- 2 threads: 1 to attach the center middle to the flower center and 1 to attach the flower center to the flower. I like high contrast for both so they pop.

Step 1. Trace the flower template onto the wrong side of the pelt (Fig. 8–1).

5"

Flower

Trace on wrong side of pelt

5½"

Fig. 8–1

STACKED & Stitched ● *Christine Morgan*

Step 2. Trace the flower middle, stem, and 2 leaf templates onto the wrong side of the Wool-Felt or chosen fabric.

> **Tip:** If you choose a fabric that will fray and/or is lightweight, fuse it to some medium weight interfacing first.

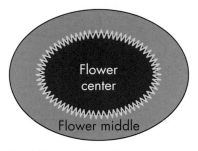

Fig. 8–2

Step 3. Trace the flower center onto the wrong side of your chosen fabric. Fuse the fabric to the interfacing first, if necessary.

Step 4. Cut out all six shapes.

Step 5. Pin the flower center to the flower middle and zigzag stitch (W 3.6, L .75). Go around twice for good coverage on raw edges and good visibility (Fig. 8–2).

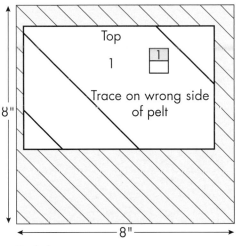

Fig. 8–3a

Step 6. Pin the assembled flower center to the flower and zigzag stitch (W 4.0, L .75); go around twice.

> **Tip:** I prefer to zigzag 2 times with a wider stitch length instead of once with a shorter stitch length to avoid the thread jamming.

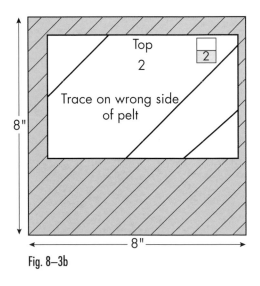

Fig. 8–3b

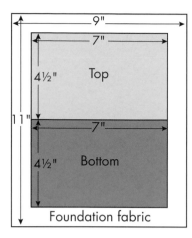

Fig. 8–4

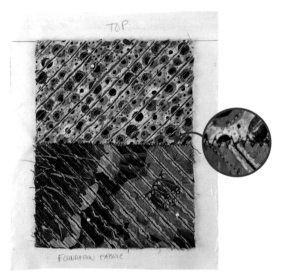

Fig. 8–5

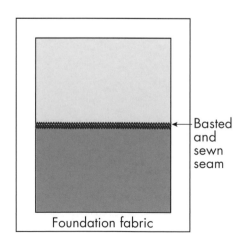

Basted and sewn seam

Foundation fabric

Fig. 8–6

2. BACKGROUND

You will need:

- ◉ 2 templates (pages 58–59)
- ◉ 2 finished, squared pelts at least 8" x 8" each
- ◉ 1 piece of foundation fabric approximately 9" x 11"
- ◉ Thread (black)

Step 1. Trace templates on the wrong sides of the pelts. The top and bottom pelts need to be cut with the rows going in opposite directions to create the chevron. Line up the 45-degree angles on the templates with the bias stitching on the pelt backs. Review Chapter 4 if you have any questions about this step (Figs. 8–3a and b, page 53).

Step 2. Cut out both background shapes.

Step 3. Draw the outline of the background on the foundation fabric (Fig. 8–4).

Step 4. Pin the background pelts to the foundation fabric and baste using a zigzag stitch (W 5.0, L 2.0) to join the seam (Fig. 8–5).

Step 5. Sew a zigzag stitch (W 4.2, L 1.2) on either side of the basted seam (Fig. 8–6).

3. FRAME

You will need:

- ⊙ 1 piece of 11" x 12" black WoolFelt

Step 1. Cut out five pieces of WoolFelt to make the frame (Fig. 8–7):

1 piece 8½" x 10½" for the back
2 pieces ¾" x 9" for top and bottom
2 pieces ¾" x 11" for sides

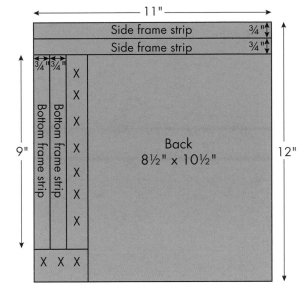

Fig. 8–7. Black WoolFelt

4. CONSTRUCTION

You will need:

- ⊙ 1 length of braid 7" for the hanger
- ⊙ The 5 frame components
- ⊙ The assembled flower, stem, and 2 leaves
- ⊙ The foundation fabric with the background pelts attached
- ⊙ Rotary cutter
- ⊙ Clear acrylic ruler
- ⊙ Thread in colors that match or are slightly darker than the flower, stem, and leaf colors
- ⊙ Thread (black)

Step 1. Position flower, stem, and leaves on the background and pin in place (Fig. 8–8).

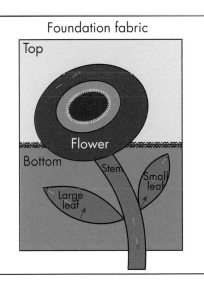

Fig. 8–8

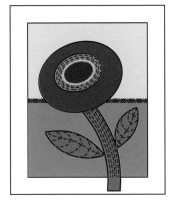

Fig. 8–9. Free-motion detail

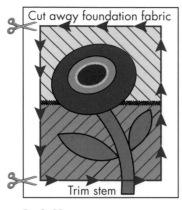

Fig. 8–10

Fig. 8–11

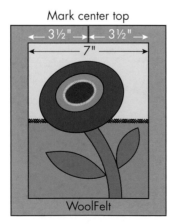

Fig. 8–12

Step 2. Attach the components to the background starting with the stem; use a zigzag stitch (W 3.2, L .50) and then attach both leaves (use the same stitch as stem). Change the thread and attach the flower (W 4.0, L .75). Go around twice.

Step 3. Drop the feed dogs, attach a walking foot, set the machine to straight stitch, and change to the thread chosen to free-motion the details in the stem, leaves, and flower parts (Fig. 8–9, page 55).

Step 4. Trim off the stem that extends into the border and then trim off all excess foundation fabric to the edge of the background (Fig. 8–10).

Tip: I like having a border, even if it will eventually be cut away, so that I can see that the foundation fabric isn't folded up and getting sewn over.

Step 5. Center the assembled and trimmed piece on the 8½" x 10½" black WoolFelt and pin it. Using a clear acrylic ruler, line up the ½" line with the edge of the background. Trim to 8" x 10" (Fig. 8–11).

Step 6. Mark the center top for hanger placement (Fig. 8–12).

STACKED & Stitched ⊚ *Christine Morgan*

Step 7. Raise the feed dogs, replace the walking foot with a regular presser foot, and change to black thread. Fold the braid in half, flatten the ends, and place them side by side. Insert the braid between the foundation fabric and the back fabric (WoolFelt) at the center top mark. Zigzag stitch (W 5.0, L 2.0) over the braid and around the perimeter (Fig. 8–13).

Fig. 8–13

Step 8. Attach the frame strips: Place a 9" x ¾" strip flush with the top edge of the back; zigzag stitch to attach (W 4.2, L 1.2). Attach the other 9" strip to the bottom and then attach both 11" x ¾" strips to either side (Fig. 8–14).

Step 9. Trim excess fabric from corners (Fig. 8–15).

Step 10. Straight stitch approximately ⅛" in from the edge all the way around (Fig. 8–16).

Fig. 8–14

Fig. 8–15

← ⅛" from edge

Fig. 8–16

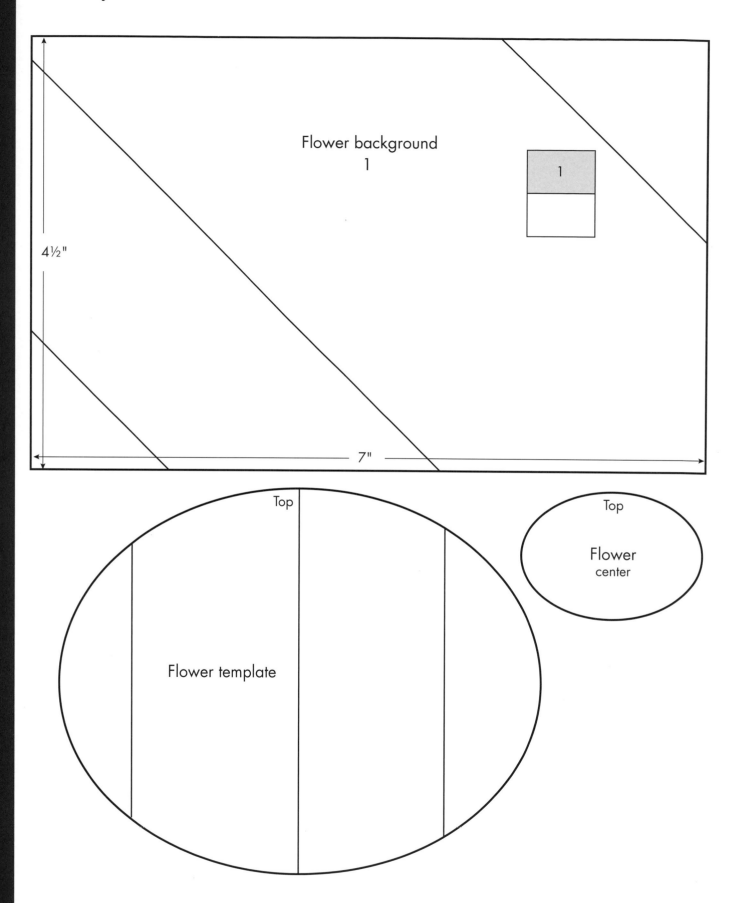

Flower background
1

1

4½"

7"

Top

Top

Flower
center

Flower template

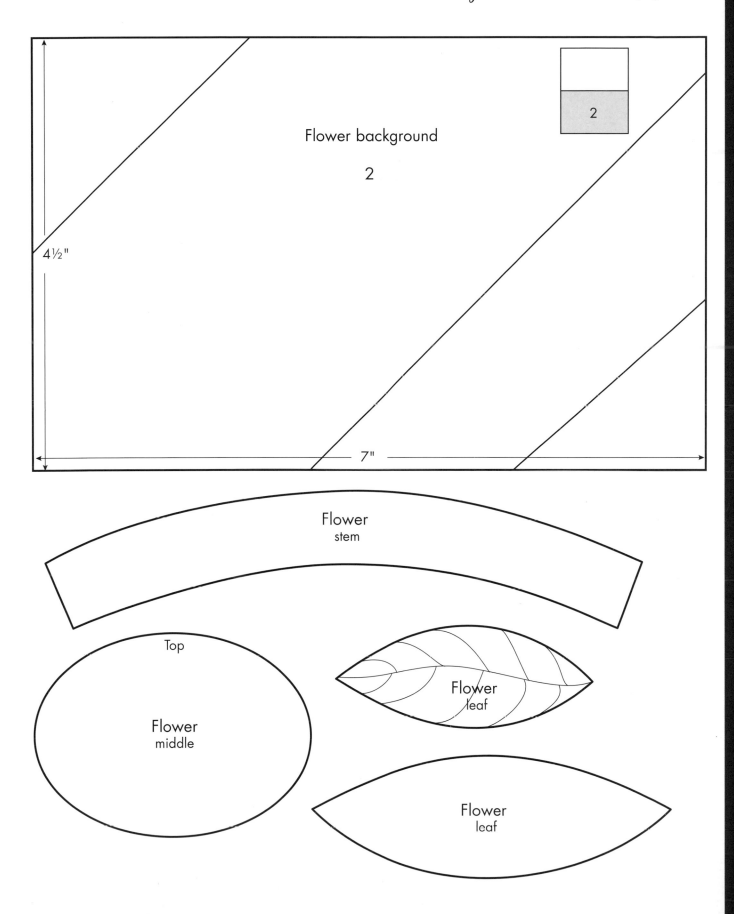

Flower background

2

4½"

7"

Flower
stem

Top

Flower
middle

Flower
leaf

Flower
leaf

Project 3: **LEAF PLACEMATS,** 20" x 14" each

Project 3: LEAF PLACEMATS

20" x 14" each (2 placemats)

It is important that all 4 pelts used in this project look good next to one another. They should have enough contrast so that the individual shapes are distinct, but because the design is nature-inspired, they don't need to be high contrast.

You will have extra pelt fabric after you have cut out the pattern pieces—approximately 8" x 12" from each pelt. I created extra-large pelts to start with because I wanted to make sure you had plenty of room; the templates are large and they need to be cut at right angles to create the chevron.

You will need:

- 2 templates (see page 65)
- 2 foundation fabrics each 15" x 21"
- 2 pieces of sturdy back fabric each 20" x 26"
- 4 pelts each approximately 14" x 18"
- Ruler
- Thread (Your choice. I like darker better than a matching or a lighter color.)

Tip: You will want to be able to wash these placemats, so prewash the foundation and back fabrics.

Project 2: Leaf Placemats

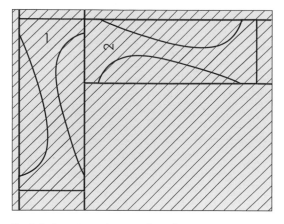

Fig. 9–1. Finish with straight edge.

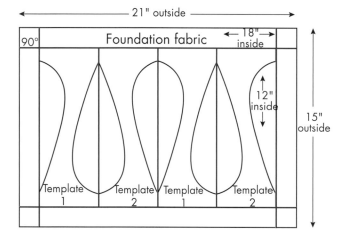

Fig. 9–2

Step 1. Trace the templates onto the wrong side of the 4 pelts. You will need 1 of each per pelt: There are 3 shapes per template for a total of 24 cut pieces. Line up the 45-degree angle on the templates with the bias stitching on the pelt back. Finish the straight lines with a ruler (Fig. 9–1).

Step 2. Cut out all 24 shapes—3 shapes from each template.

Step 3. Draw the designs on the foundation fabrics. Establish the right angle of the left side and top, and then trace the templates to complete the drawing (Fig. 9–2).

Step 4. Arrange pieces to your liking. The configuration in diagram 3 worked well for me (Fig. 9–3).

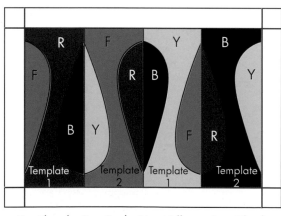
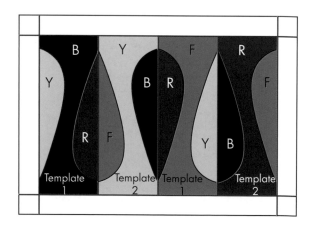

F= Floral, R = Red, Y = Yellow, B = Black

Fig. 9–3

STACKED & Stitched ● *Christine Morgan*

Step 5. When you are satisfied with your arrangement, pin the shapes to the foundation fabrics and baste using a zigzag stitch (W 5.0, L 2.0). Start with the center seam and work out to either side. Keep everything flat, make sure your pieces are correctly lined up, and remove pins as you go to prevent distortion (Fig. 9–4).

Fig. 9–4. Pelt pieces are basted to the foundation fabric.

Step 6. Sew using a zigzag stitch (W 4.2, L 1.2) on either side of all basted seams (Fig. 9–5).

Step 7. Iron the wrong side of both placemats to ease any puckering.

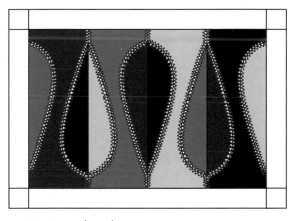

Fig. 9–5. Basted and sewn

Step 8. Zigzag stitch (W 5.0, L 2.0) around the perimeters of both placemats. Trim excess foundation fabric to ⅞" so that 1" border will extend ⅛" in from the center of the perimeter stitching (Fig. 9–6).

Step 9. Center and pin the placemats on their respective back fabrics making sure both the placemat and the back fabric are smooth and flat. Straight stitch all the straight seams starting in the center and working out to the sides. Straight stitch around the perimeter going through the center of the perimeter zigzag stitching you did in step 8 (Fig. 9–7, page 64).

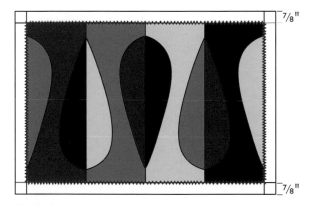

Fig. 9–6

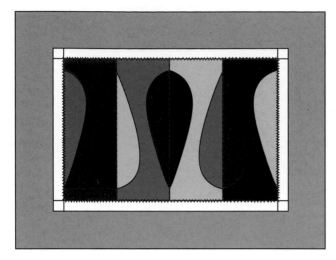

Fig. 9–7

Step 10. Mark 1" fold lines on all sides. Trim excess back fabric (Fig. 9–8).

Step 11. Iron fold lines, miter corners, and pin in place. Back fabric should overlap the edge of the placemat, partially or completely covering the perimeter zigzag stitching. Zigzag stitch (W 4.0, L 1.2) the border down as shown in figure 9–9.

Step 12. Hand stitch the mitered corners closed.

The table runner is made just like the placemats. Just make additional pelts. Note that the length has to be multiples of 4½" (Fig. 9–10, page 65).

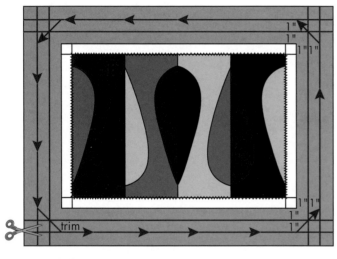

Fig. 9–8

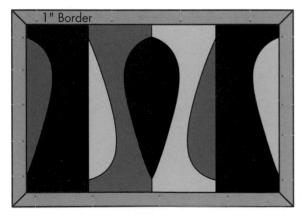

Fig. 9–9

STACKED & Stitched ⬤ *Christine Morgan*

Fig. 9–10. Construct the table runner as you would the placemats.

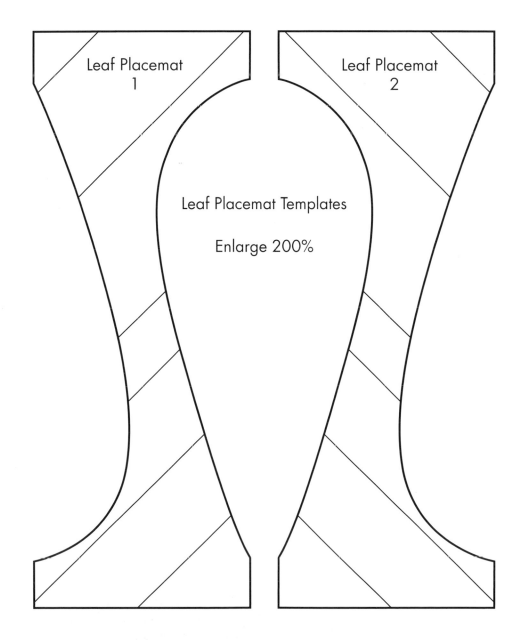

Leaf Placemat
1

Leaf Placemat
2

Leaf Placemat Templates

Enlarge 200%

Project 4: RED POPPY PILLOW, 24" x 12"

I have included this project because it is the design about which I receive the most compliments and questions. It may appear complicated, but taken step by step for each part, you will find it is fairly simple.

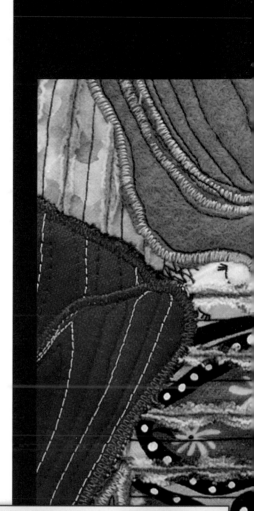

Project 4: RED POPPY PILLOW

24" x 12"

I have organized the construction into 7 parts:

1. **Flower Centers**
2. **Flower Petals**
3. **Assemble Flowers**
4. **Stems, Leaves, Sepals, and Bud**
5. **Background**
6. **Assemble Pillow Top**
7. **Assemble Pillow**

1. FLOWER CENTERS

You will need: (Fig. 10–1)

- 4 templates (page 76)
- 3" x 8" flower center fabric (medium olive/brown faux-suede)
- 3" x 8" backing for flower center (optional; use backing if the fabric you choose has a tendency to pucker)
- 3" x 5" flower center middle fabric (dark brown textured faux-suede)
- Thread (golden yellow)

Fig. 10–1. To make the flower centers you will need templates, fabric, and thread.

Step 1. Trace the flower center templates on the right side of the fabric (medium brown faux-suede). Trace 2 templates of A and C and 1 of B.

Fig. 10–2

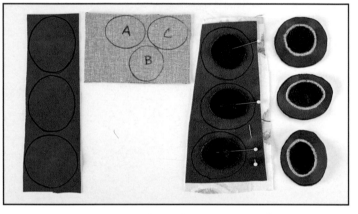

Fig. 10–3. Steps 1 through 5 create the flower centers.

Fig. 10–4. To make the flower petals you will need templates, fabric, felt, and 2 threads.

Step 2. Trace the flower center middle on the wrong side of the fabric (dark-brown textured)—2 of A/C and 1 of B. Cut out all 3 shapes.

Step 3. Place the backing fabric behind the flower center fabric (if the fabric you have chosen tends to pucker) and pin the flower center middles in place.

Step 4. Zigzag stitch (W 4.0, L .75) using golden-yellow thread around the flower center middle. Go around 2 or 3 times until you have good coverage of the raw edge (Fig. 10–2).

Step 5. Cut out all three completed flower centers. See Fig. 10–3.

2. FLOWER PETALS

You will need: (Fig. 10–4)

- 7 templates (see pages 76–77)
- 14" x 14" piece of red fabric
- 14" x 14" piece of thin red felt (instead of white batting)
- Thread
    red (darker than the red fabric)
    bright yellow

Step 1. Trace the flower petal templates onto the right side of the red fabric (Fig. 10–5, page 69).

STACKED & Stitched ⊙ *Christine Morgan*

Step 2. Pin the red felt to the wrong side of the red fabric.

Step 3. Free-motion quilt the petals: Drop the feed dogs, attach a walking foot, and set your machine to straight stitch. Using bright yellow thread, outline a petal shape and then add the veining. Outline and vein all of the petals. Don't overdo the yellow veining, as you will add red veining in Step 4 (Fig. 10–6).

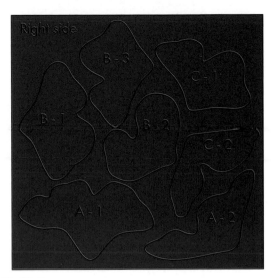

Fig. 10–5

> **Tip:** If you haven't done much free-motion quilting, practice on scrap fabric until you are comfortable. It is easier to add veining if you keep the top of the petal shape towards you and move fluidly back and forth.

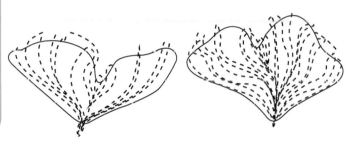

Fig. 10–6. Free-motion veining

Step 4. Switch to red thread and add red veining in all petals (Figs. 10–7a and b).

Fig. 10–7a. One petal has been outlined and yellow-veined. A second petal has been outlined and partially yellow-veined.

Fig. 10–7b. Remember to use a darker red thread than the fabric for the red veining.

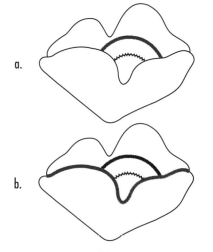

Fig. 10–8. Flowers A, B, and C pinned together, and an example of a completed flower

3. ASSEMBLE FLOWERS

You will need:

- ◉ 7 flower petals
- ◉ 3 flower centers
- ◉ Thread

   red (this red should match your red fabric as closely as possible)

   dark brown (this thread should match your flower center middle fabric)

Step 1. Pin corresponding petals and centers together to form flowers A, B, and C (Fig. 10–8).

Step 2. Raise the feed dogs and replace the walking foot with a regular presser foot. Using dark-brown thread, zigzag stitch (W 3.4, L .50) the flower centers to the petals. Attach all three flower centers. (Fig. 10–9a)

Step 3. Switch to red thread and zigzag stitch (W 3.4, L .75) where the petals overlap. Zigzag stitch (W 3.2, L .50) over the same area to get good coverage on raw edges (Fig. 10–9b).

Step 4. Cut away excess fabric from the back of finished flowers, especially from the center of flower B to reduce bulk when you add free-motion detail later.

Fig. 10–9a and b. Satin stitch edges

4. STEMS, LEAVES, SEPALS, AND BUD

You will need: (Fig. 10–10)
- 11 templates (page 77)
- 12" x 12" piece of WoolFelt

Fig. 10–10. You will need templates and WoolFelt to make the rest of the flowers.

I used a moss green WoolFelt lightly sprayed with a diluted bleach solution (6 parts water to 1 part bleach). Have a bucket of cool soapy water ready to submerge the fabric to stop the bleaching process. Rinse well, line dry, and iron.

Step 1. Trace all of the templates on the wrong side of the felt and mark as shown (Fig. 10–11).

Step 2. Cut out all shapes.

Fig. 10–11. Trace all of the flowers parts on the Wool-Felt.

5. BACKGROUND

You will need: (Fig. 10–12)
- Template
- 4 pelts at least 9" x 9"
- 15" x 27" foundation fabric
- Thread (dark green)

Step 1. Use a finished flower and a felt stem or leaf to audition fabrics against the background pelts. Make sure all your fabrics look good together and that your stems, leaves, etc., show up against the background.

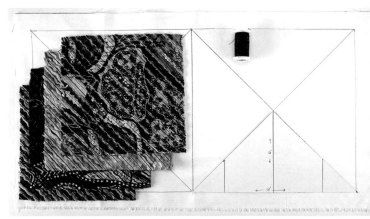

Fig. 10–12. To complete the project you will need pelts, a template, foundation fabric, and thread.

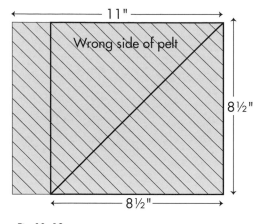

Fig. 10–13

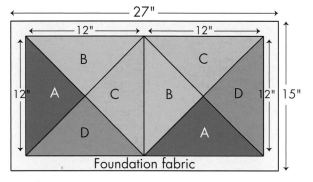

Fig. 10–14

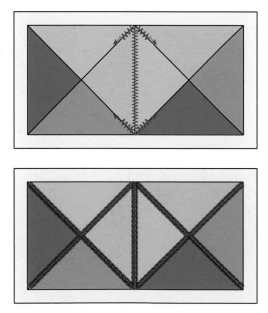

Fig. 10–15. Basted and sewn

Step 2. Make four pelts with your chosen top fabrics. You will need to cut 2 triangle templates from each pelt, so you will need a minimum of 4 squares 8½" x 8½".

Step 3. Trace the triangle template twice on the wrong side of each of the pelts. You need 8 triangles total (Fig. 10–13).

Step 4. Draw the design on the foundation fabric.

Step 5. Decide where you want to place your background triangles (Fig. 10–14).

Step 6. Pin the pelt triangles to the foundation fabric (3 pins per triangle should be adequate).

Step 7. Using dark green thread, baste (zigzag stitch W 5.0, L 2.0) all of the seams, starting with the center seam and working away from the center. Remove pins as you go.

Step 8. Sew (zigzag stitch W 4.2, L 1.2) on either side of the basted seams (Fig. 10–15).

Step 9. Iron the back of the foundation fabric to ease any minor puckering.

6: ASSEMBLE PILLOW TOP

You will need:

- 3 assembled flowers (A, B, and C)
- Stems, leaves, sepals, and bud
- Completed (basted and sewn) background
- Thread

  golden yellow (This thread does not have to match your stem, leaf, fabric color, etc., but should help to define the shapes by contrasting with the background fabric.)

  red (The same used to assemble the flowers.)

  dark green (The same thread used in basting and sewing before. This is the thread you will be using to free-motion stitch the detail of your stems, etc., so it should have strong contrast to those fabrics.)

Step 1. Pin all of the components in place. Use just a pin or two in each as you will have to remove or hold aside some pieces to sew others in place. Use figure 10–16 as a placement guide.

Step 2. Using golden-yellow thread, zigzag stitch (W 3.0, L .50) all of the stems to the background. Start with the stem for the bud, and then attach the rest of the stems (the bud stem goes behind the stem for flower A). Attach all of the leaves. Attach the bud and bud sepal.

Step 3. Switch to red thread. Check the positions of the flowers and pin them securely in place. Zigzag stitch (W 3.4, L .75) around the

Fig. 10–16. This is the result of steps 1–7. Label the flowers and bud when placing them for reference.

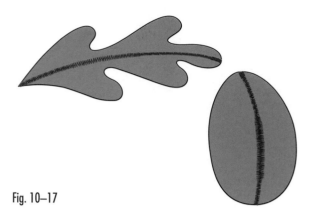

Fig. 10–17

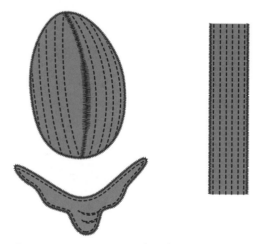

Fig. 10–18. Free motion details

flowers. Zigzag stitch (W 3.2, L .50) over the same areas, focusing on covering any raw edge.

Step 4. Switch to golden-yellow thread and zigzag stitch (W 3.0, L .50) to attach the sepals for flowers A and C. Add center veins to the leaves and bud. Narrow and widen stitch length as shown (Fig. 10–17).

Step 5. Switch to dark green thread. Drop the feed dogs, attach a walking foot, and set the machine to straight stitch. Free-motion stitch the details on stems, leaves, sepals, and flower centers (Fig. 10–18).

Step 6. Trim stems where they extend beyond the border.

Step 7. Raise the feed dogs and replace the walking foot with a regular presser foot. Zigzag stitch (W 5.0, L 2.0) around the perimeter of the pillow top.

7. ASSEMBLE PILLOW

You will need:

- 12" x 24" pillow form
- 15" x 27" fabric for pillow back
- Finished pillow top
- Thread
    black
    thread that matches the pillow back
    to hand sew closed

STACKED & Stitched ● *Christine Morgan*

Step 1. Pin the pillow top and pillow back right sides together (Fig. 10–19).

Step 2. With the wrong side of the pillow top facing up, straight stitch (L 2.0) in the center of the perimeter zigzag stitching.

Step 3. To prevent fraying, zigzag stitch (W 5.0, L 1.5) just outside the straight stitching you did in step 2. Overlapping the perimeter zigzag stitching should stabilize the pillow back and foundation fabrics (Fig. 10–20), or, use a serger.

Step 4. Trim excess fabric from top and sides as shown (Fig. 10–21).

Step 5. Turn the finished pillowcase right-side out, poking out the corners (I use the rounded end of an old artist's brush).

Step 6. Insert a pillow form and hand stitch the open seam closed.

You did it! Cue the Hallelujah Chorus! I forgive you for all the horrible things you may have thought and/or said about me during the construction of this pillow. Thanks for hanging in there!!

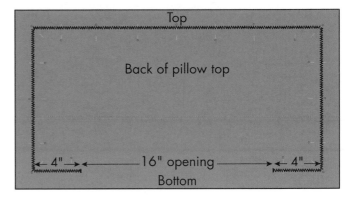

Fig. 10–19

Fig. 10–20. Stabilizing raw edge or use serger

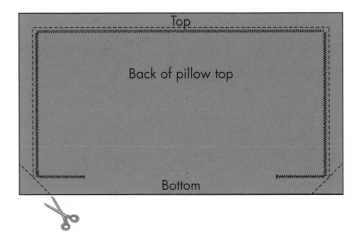

Fig. 10–21

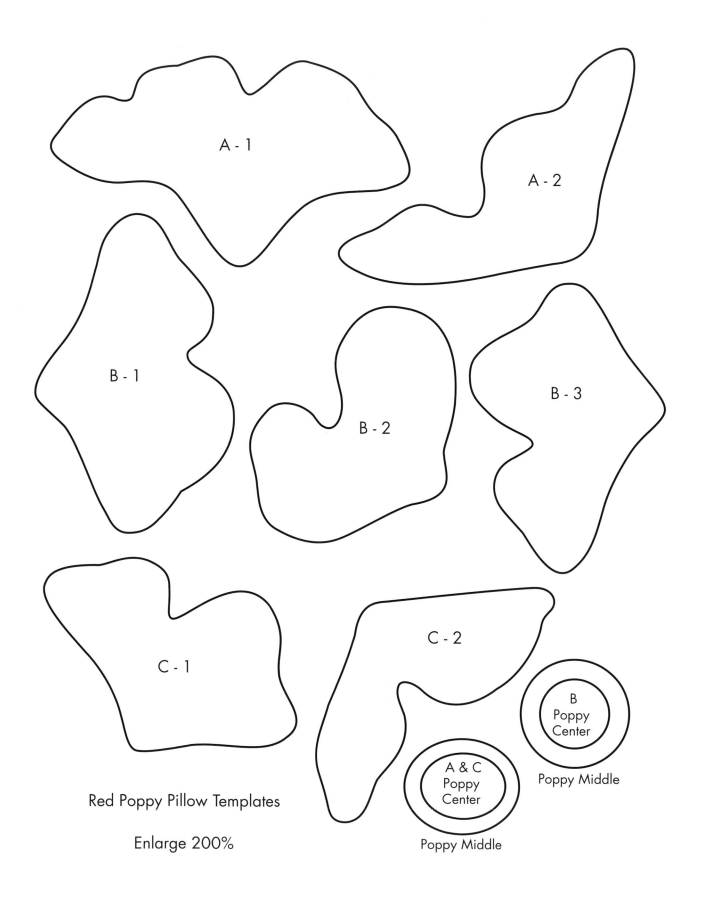

A - 1

A - 2

B - 1

B - 2

B - 3

C - 1

C - 2

B
Poppy
Center

Poppy Middle

A & C
Poppy
Center

Poppy Middle

Red Poppy Pillow Templates

Enlarge 200%

Red Poppy Pillow Templates

Enlarge 200%

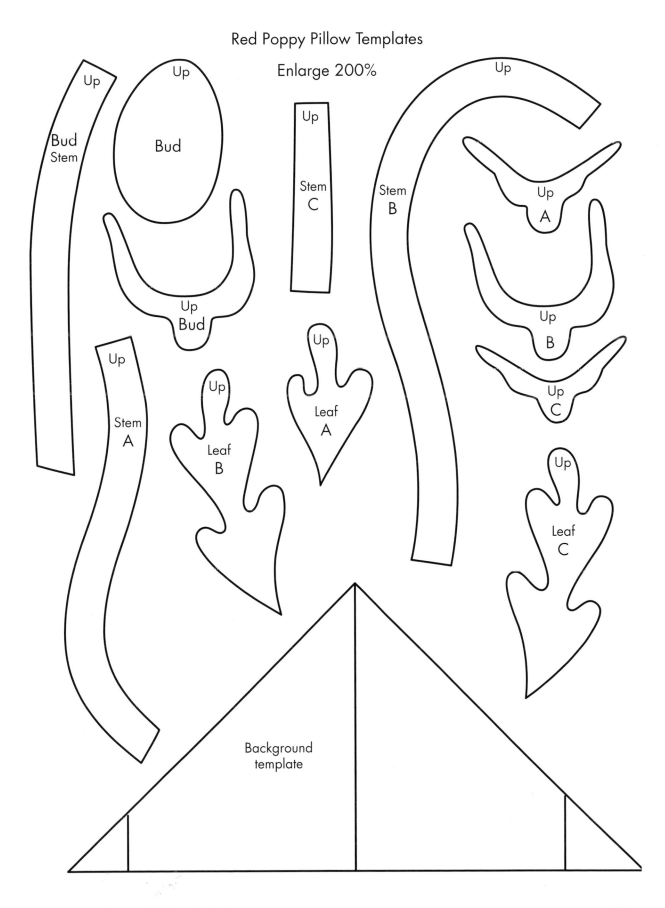

STACKED & Stitched ● Christine Morgan

About
Christine Morgan

PHOTO: Geffrey E. Stauffer

My husband and I live in a small but charming circa 1830s farmhouse in the Susquehanna River hills near Lancaster, Pennsylvania. We are surrounded by beautiful scenery and a rich history in textiles.

I am inspired by nature every day and have always been drawn to the incredible variety of patterns, colors, and textures of bugs, leaves, and bark. The closer you look, the more you see. I like feeling close to nature and a part of the natural world.

I have studied both commercial and fine art, but I think of myself as a decorative artist and I enjoy creating things that people live with and touch.

My studio is in the summer kitchen and I get a thrill every time I walk through the door. There is no place I would rather be and I am very grateful to have found something that I love to do.

If you want to chat, you may contact me at:
fiberworks@comcast.net.

Opposite: Flower Wallhanging Variation, detail

more AQS Books

This is only a small selection of the books available from the American Quilter's Society. AQS books are known worldwide for timely topics, clear writing, beautiful color photos, and accurate illustrations and patterns. The following books are available from your local bookseller, quilt shop, or public library.

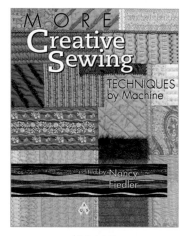

#8667

#8671

#8532

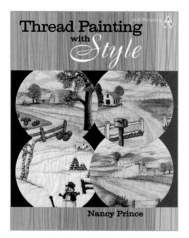

#8354

#8763

#8529

#8528

#8664

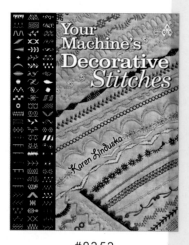

#8353